LENT TALKS

LENT TALKS

Preparing for Easter with Radio 4

BBC Radio 4

First published in Great Britain in 2017

Society for Promoting Christian Knowledge
36 Causton Street
London SW1P 4ST
www.spck.org.uk

British Library Cataloguing-in-Publication Data
A catalogue record for this book is available from the British Library

ISBN 978–0–281–07863–9
eBook ISBN 978–0–281–07870–7

Typeset by Fakenham Prepress Solutions, Fakenham, Norfolk NR21 8NN
Manufacture managed by Jellyfish
First printed in Great Britain by CPI
Subsequently digitally printed in Great Britain

eBook by Fakenham Prepress Solutions, Fakenham, Norfolk NR21 8NN

Produced on paper from sustainable forests

Contents

Foreword

Stories provide a vehicle for learning about life, its richness and its depths, but when stories become too familiar, there is a risk that they cease to have the impact on us they had when we first encountered them. That's even true of the stories of the temptation, trials and death of Jesus Christ – stories that have been told over and over throughout the season of Lent for two millennia now.

What the BBC Radio 4 *Lent Talks* do each year is retell those stories through the eyes and experiences of a series of stimulating contemporary speakers and writers. Listening to them tell of their thoughts and feelings, passions and reflections, we see how those familiar stories play out in and resonate with the lives of individuals from our own time. In this way, key events in the life of Jesus take on a vivid, up-to-date dimension.

At the heart of the season of Lent is a story that is dramatic and rich in themes, but it's not an easy setting for a non-Christian audience: self-denial, introspection, temptation, betrayal and abandonment against a background of supernatural events. Yet Lent is a season that encompasses some of the most profound dimensions of the human condition, and these talks help to bring that home. As with so many things in life that are demanding or require perseverance, Lent can be a time of increased self-knowledge.

For a broadcaster, the challenge is to speak to a general audience that consists of people of all faiths and none, and so the group of writers in this book represent a rich mix to illuminate the themes. In broadcast terms, such 'single-voice' talks can be the hardest thing to get right. The presenter has to hold the listeners' attention for 14 minutes with an engaging style and delivery and, most important, offer something that will linger in the mind long after the broadcast has ended.

This volume offers some vivid examples of that. The writer, director and literary curator James Runcie, author of the series The Grantchester Mysteries, draws on his know-how as a crime writer to view Christ's Passion in the light of that expertise. He says, 'Crime writing . . . gives the author the opportunity to put characters under extreme pressure and see how they react to the continual threat of death and disaster'.

The playwright Bonnie Greer reflects on Jesus' silence before Pilate and asks, 'Why did he not defend himself?' She finds an answer in the story of the character Solomon Northrup in *12 Years a Slave*, who demonstrates the power of silence to name one's own terms. She concludes, 'there is power, too, in not speaking'.

Ann Widdecombe explores the events from the perspective of a politician. She contemplates the business of making choices that are freely, bravely arrived at. She suggests that Jesus, in his decision to go to the cross and the devastating effect of that on his family and friends, offers a fearful reminder that 'we must be prepared to let people down, to disappoint those whom we love, to refuse to live up to the expectations of others if by doing so we do what is right.'

For a while, Giles Fraser thought that he might become a chaplain in the army. It was a daunting call and, reflecting on it in the 2010 series, he dwells on what might be asked of him and whether or not his faith would survive the first-hand experience of so much suffering in what he likens to a parallel of Christ's Holy Week, which is 'a searching audit of our moral courage'.

Alexander McCall Smith, the author of The No. 1 Ladies' Detective Agency series, taps into the abandonment many feel when they get older and ponders what Christianity has to say about fairness and forgiveness. Nick Baines, writing against the backdrop of the 2011 riots in Croydon, where he had been bishop, explores 'how we live with ourselves and one another; how we love and hate; who we love and hate' and the values and core beliefs that reflect and challenge both the individual and the community.

Lent is a season that showcases the strengths and frailties of humanity. It explores the reason we're alive here today. It is a time of temptation and trial that confronts us with how we must wrestle with what is ahead and prepare ourselves perhaps to be tested to the limit. But it is also a time of reassurance for humanity. For those seeking a spiritual connection with God, it offers ways to discover his purposes and the way we should live them out. Lent, with the increased self-knowledge it can bring, can be a time of growth. In these talks, present-day voices offer new insights into profound new ideas. They signpost ways to recognize the pitfalls ahead. They give permission for us to accept that some things are hard and demand perseverance. Even in the face of failure, they tell us, there is new wisdom to be found that may be ultimately more far-reaching. And success may take shapes it is hard for us to recognize at the outset. The words of these Lent talks offer a kind of nourishment. This book is a feast for the contemporary soul.

Christine Morgan
Head of Radio, BBC Religion and Ethics

WHETHER WE APPRECIATE
THE STORY OF THE PASSION
AS DIVINE REVELATION
OR SIMPLY AS POETRY OR
METAPHOR – IT IS THE
ARCHETYPAL PRESENTATION
OF THE ULTIMATE 'MYSTERY
DRAMA': THE MYSTERY
OF WHAT IT MEANS TO
BE ALIVE.

Week One: Mystery

James Runcie

First broadcast on BBC Radio 4 on 25 February 2015

James Runcie is a writer, director and literary curator. He is the author of the series The Grantchester Mysteries, a Fellow of the Royal Society of Literature, Visiting Professor at Bath Spa University and the Commissioning Editor for Arts at BBC Radio 4. He was a founder member of The Late Show and made documentary films for the BBC for 15 years. He then went freelance to make programmes for Channel 4 and ITV. He was Artistic Director of the Bath Literature Festival from 2010 to 2013 and Head of Literature at the Southbank Centre in London from 2013 to 2015.

Back in 2010 I started to write a series of detective novels with the provisional title The Grantchester Mysteries. The stories begin in an English village in 1953 – when the death penalty was still extant, homosexuality was illegal and human relationships were probably conducted in a more private manner than they are in our contemporary world of relentless self-disclosure.

What I wanted to do was tell a tale of post-war Britain using the mystery story as a framework. It was to be an account of social and ethical change – with murder, theft, betrayal and injustice.

Crime writing is helpful for this. It gives the author the opportunity to put characters under extreme pressure and see how they react to the continual threat of death and disaster.

The precariousness of the human condition, the awareness of time and mortality, and the ability to react to abrupt shifts in fortune, whether good or bad, are paramount. They would be morality tales, parables even, aiming for the economy of storytelling found in the Bible; meditations on the sin and suffering that underpin religious thinking, particularly in Lent.

When I began to plan the stories I realized that the central character could easily have been a doctor or a teacher, but I chose a priest. I wanted someone with easy access to personal secrets; present at key moments of birth, marriage and death; someone who also had sufficient freedom of movement to go where the police could not.

I also wanted religion to be taken seriously as a subject. I hoped to escape the sitcom clichés of *All Gas and Gaiters* and *Bless Me, Father* and to have, as the main character, a questioning, thoughtful Church of England vicar – rather than the kind once played by Derek Nimmo, Dick Emery or Rowan Atkinson, the latter in *Four Weddings and a Funeral*. That didn't mean comedy would not have its place, but it would be a world in which the comic and the tragic, the profound and the trivial could exist side by side. This genre of writing is often belittled as 'cosy crime' – historically these are stories in which one doesn't need to worry too much about the graphic depiction of the violence found in 'hard-boiled' alternatives – and, indeed, in the Bible. 'Cosy crime' is not a term I like very much. One has to remember that under the cosy, the pot may be scalding and the tea poisoned. Violence, and the consequences of crime, cannot be ignored so easily.

Having decided on the fictional character (Canon Sidney Chambers) and a real setting (the village of Grantchester, just outside Cambridge) one of the most vital things I had to do was find a tone the reader could trust and feel at home with.

One way of doing this is to see how others have done it before. And so I looked to the past, particularly to novels that featured clergymen or people of faith – the work of Trollope, Dostoevsky, Dorothy L. Sayers and G. K. Chesterton. In all of them there is a natural authority. Even if the writer claims to be mystified by the events that are being revealed, the authorial voice dominates the material. Clarity and confidence matter.

There was then the small matter of plot.

In 1929, Ronald Knox, a Catholic priest and author of *The Viaduct Murder*, *The Body in the Silo* and *Still Dead*, advised that a detective story:

> must have as its main interest the unravelling of a mystery; a mystery whose elements are clearly presented to the reader at an early stage in the proceedings, and whose nature is

such as to arouse *curiosity*, a curiosity which is gratified at
the end.

He came up with what he called 'The Ten Commandments' of
writing a detective story. Here are just five of them:

1   the criminal must be mentioned in the early part of the story
    but must not be anyone whose thoughts the reader has been
    allowed to know;
2   the detective himself must not commit the crime;
3   not more than one secret room or passage is allowable;
4   twin brothers, and doubles generally, must not appear unless
    we have been duly prepared for them; and, bizarrely:
5   no Chinaman must figure in the story!

While taking heed of some of his advice (twins *are* a definite
no-no – far too obvious), I also turned back to a much earlier
form of mystery drama for inspiration: the religious plays of the
thirteenth and fourteenth centuries.

The English mystery cycles were popular broad-brush representations of key biblical scenes, told by the people and for the
people. Performed in English rather than Latin, these dramatic
representations were taken out of the churches and into the streets.
They were staged in tents and carts and on makeshift stages for
promenade performances in town centres and around cathedrals.
Often taking place on the feast of Corpus Christi, between late
May and early June, they featured a series of short scenes, from the
Creation of the World until Doomsday, involving speech, dialogue,
music, dancing, special effects and even wrestling. Four complete

series of these plays – what would today be called the 'DVD boxed sets' – survive, from Chester, Towneley, York and Coventry.

As in the contemporary mystery drama, the focus is on human fallibility. Whether it be temptation, fear or pure evil, crime is never far away. Take Cain's murder of Abel, Lamech's killing of Cain, Abraham's near miss with Isaac or Herod's Massacre of the Innocents. The stories chosen mixed murder with morality, so by the time the narrative reached the Passion of Christ, audiences were well attuned to a multi-genre mixture of tension, mystery and revelation.

Imagine it on film. A close-up of a bare and twisted tree. A wide shot of the hot and dusty road to Jerusalem. High sun, baked earth.

The structure of these stories has an archetypal timelessness, so much so that looking at the Easter story through the prism of mystery drama, it is extraordinary how clearly biblical events follow the methodology of a contemporary thriller.

Imagine it on film. A close-up of a bare and twisted tree. A wide shot of the hot and dusty road to Jerusalem. High sun, baked earth. It's a bit like a Western. In the distance we see 12 men, a gang of insurgents, with their charismatic leader, tired and struggling. They've been on the road a long time. The camera lingers on one of the men. We think it might be Jesus, but it's not. It is Judas, an early version of the police informer.

Before they enter Jerusalem, the characters make camp and tell each other a series of stories so the audience can get to know

Jesus warns that the Temple will be destroyed within three days. This instituties the ticking-clock scenario, the race against time: when, how and why will the Temple be destroyed - or can it be saved?

them. There are a few minor crimes and petty thefts: the stealing of an ass – and a colt; the wanton destruction of a fig tree. On reaching the city there's a bit of a scuffle with the scribes, Pharisees and hypocrites. The gang approach the Temple and attack the money changers. It's like a heist movie except there's a twist: the gang don't take the loot.

What are they after? Something bigger, more political, religious – something no one can understand. It's a mystery.

Jesus warns that the Temple will be destroyed within three days. This institutes the ticking-clock scenario, the race against time: when, how and why will the Temple be destroyed – or can it be saved?

You've got three days.

The story now switches to focus on the panic amongst the city's religious and business leaders. This is the threatened establishment. They have to move fast to protect their own interests. They meet up to discuss ways in which they can restore order and get rid of the troublemakers – legally or illegally.

This initiates the murder plot.

They decide to infiltrate the gang. They find Judas. He's the mole, the snitch, the rat – paid with blood money to let the forces of law and order know when and where Jesus can be kidnapped.

Jesus calls his supporters together and, in the kind of upper room of a restaurant where a group of Mafiosi might meet, he tells his people of a conspiracy theory.

His behaviour is unsettling. He talks enigmatically. He has had visions. He is, perhaps, a little paranoid – convinced that his best-loved disciple will abandon him.

The next scene ratchets up the tension and takes place, as in all good film noir, at night.

Christ is alone and unguarded in a remote location that's hard to protect – a garden. A group of vigilantes arrive, together with the chief priests and the elders of the Temple. Judas is in their midst. The camera stays on him for the kiss of betrayal; we cut to Jesus' reaction; he is led away. A reaction shot shows the disciples left in disarray in the dark.

Under unofficial arrest, Jesus endures a mock trial in which he is 'fitted up' by two false witnesses. He is accused of blasphemy and beaten up.

Now there's a switch of genre. The story becomes a traditional courtroom drama. Pontius Pilate washes his hands of the whole event, submits to popular pressure, organizes an exchange of prisoners and issues the death sentence. In the words of Matthew's Gospel, 'See ye to it' (Matthew 27.24 AV).

It's all over. Except that it isn't. Like all good mystery drama, there has to be a final reel, an Act 5, a twist.

We then cut to a Tarantino-style bloodbath finale. In prison, Christ is beaten and tortured. There is no last-minute reprieve; he is crucified. Two thieves die with him. Judas hangs himself. The veil of the Temple is torn in two. We see the face of Christ. Rain. Cut back wide. Lightning. Fade to black. Credits.

It's all over.

Except that it isn't.

Like all good mystery drama, there has to be a final reel, an Act 5, a twist – and in the drama of the Passion there are three.

Twist one: the body disappears. In this ultimate version of a 'locked-room mystery', Jesus, who is officially dead, manages to escape from a sealed tomb that's guarded by soldiers 24 hours a day. How has he done this?

Twist two: the revelation of the murderer. In all the night-time confusion of the drama, the viewer is left wondering who is ultimately responsible for Christ's death; is it Caiaphas, Herod, Judas, Pontius Pilate or the soldiers who nailed him to the cross? Could any of these suspects admit their guilt or become the solution to the mystery?

Well, it turns out that *none* of them can claim responsibility because all of these actions were plotted by an overarching mastermind who has been behind the whole thing all along. That mastermind is, of course, God.

This is the plain and shocking truth of the Passion.

God is the murderer of Jesus. He may not have physically nailed his Son to the cross, but death was inevitable.

'For God loved the world so much that he gave his one and only Son, so that everyone who believes in him will not perish but have eternal life' (John 3.16 NLT).

This leads to . . .

Twist three: it's not death, but life. The final twist is one of transformation. The mystery genre is subverted. Through the resurrection we have a happy ending; tragedy is transformed into what, in its broadest sense, we can call a comedy, the happy ending that is the salvation of mankind.

In St Paul's words:

> Behold, I shew you *a mystery*; We shall not all sleep, but we shall all be changed, In a moment, in the twinkling of an eye, at the last trump: for the trumpet shall sound, and the dead shall be raised incorruptible, and we shall be changed.
> (1 Corinthians 15.51–52 AV)

Whereas crime drama often depends on the resolution of the narrative – with all the loose ends being tied up – this is a tale of redemption that throws its final responsibility back on to the reader.

For this is not just a story of what happens to other people; it is about what happens to us once we have become, through the simple act of reading and being mortal, an accessory to the crime.

We shall be changed.

The reader of the Gospels, like the audience at the mystery plays, becomes *part* of the narrative – left to decide if this experience is fiction or, in fact, true reality.

Can *you* believe it?

Whatever we end up deciding – whether we appreciate the story of the Passion as divine revelation or simply as poetry or metaphor – it is the archetypal presentation of the ultimate 'mystery drama': the mystery of what it means to be alive.

WEEK ONE: MYSTERY
QUESTIONS FOR REFLECTION

- How helpful do you find looking at the Passion through the lens of 'mystery drama'?
- Does it make you notice something in the Easter narrative that you didn't before?
- Which character in the story do you identify with most?
- What do you make of the evocative phrase 'God is the murderer of Jesus'?

- This tale of redemption throws its final responsibility back on the reader. How, if at all, have you changed in the light of what Christ has done for us? What areas of our lives might still need to change this Lent time?

JESUS, SILENT BEFORE
PILATE, TEACHES US THAT
POWER NEED NOT REST IN
THE ABILITY TO DICTATE
THE REALITY OF ANOTHER
PERSON OR THE ABILITY
TO CONTROL A NATION
DETERMINED TO DEFINE ITS
OWN DESTINY IN ITS OWN
TIME.

Week Two: Names

Bonnie Greer

First broadcast on BBC Radio 4 on 12 March 2014

Bonnie Greer OBE *is an American-British playwright, novelist and critic who has lived in the UK since 1986. She has appeared as a panellist on television programmes such as* Newsnight Review *and* Question Time *and has served on the boards of several leading arts organizations, including the British Museum, the Royal Opera House and the London Film School. She is also the Chancellor of Kingston University in Kingston upon Thames.*

In the late 1980s, when I still lived in New York City, some friends and I decided to bring a play over for the Edinburgh Festival.

For my friends, it would be their first trip outside of the States. No one in their families had ever been abroad. Our families and our ancestors just didn't have the freedom of movement. We black people were restricted from going where we wanted to either by law or by custom.

That was our history.

So this trip to Scotland was all very exciting and we were brimming with things that we wanted to do.

We, my friends and I, were all in the theatre, so one thing we wanted to do was a bit of 'living theatre' while in Scotland. The idea was to do something that seemed real to another person and – we hoped – make that person see the world in another way, change his or her perception.

We decided on this: we would pretend to be American heirs. We were coming to Scotland to look over our individual inheritances.

And if we could claim them, we would claim them.

So we bought a bit of tartan, made it into scarves and we were ready to roll.

We decided – being New Yorkers – that the first person to be a part of our little experiment would be a taxi driver; taxi drivers can usually spot an 'act' in the back of their cab. If it worked with the driver, then maybe we could go Scotland-wide, take a little theatre back to Manhattan.

We landed, made our way to Waverley Station and hailed a taxi. The streets were teeming, as they always are during the Festival, but the driver who picked us up took the time to be friendly and very chatty.

Eventually he got around to the question I suppose everyone in Edinburgh asks a stranger there in August: 'Are you doing a play or are you visiting?'

We were ready.

'Oh, we aren't coming to do a show,' Bobby replied, 'we've come to claim our inheritances.'

I said, 'We thought this would be a good time. I know people are probably on vacation in August, but, hey, we've got nothing to lose, plus we can get to see some plays and stuff, have a good time.' My other friend, Dana, said, 'We're in the theatre in New York, so we'd really love to see Scottish theatre, see what you guys do over here . . . while . . . we claim our inheritances.'

I think that the silence from the driver lasted about five minutes.

If it didn't, it felt that way.

He stared briefly at us in his mirror. You could see his mind working, the words running through his head: 'our inheritances'?

'Oh?' he finally said quietly.

'Yep,' my friend said.

And then we did our real street theatre bit, the *pièce de résistance*. We pulled out our passports and showed them to him.

Pointing to me, my friend Bobby said, 'She's Greer, I'm McGregor and she's Ferguson. That's our names.'

The poor driver tried to move the subject on, but I think he was just too stunned to say anything coherent.

I would have loved to have heard what he said at the supper table that night!

★ ★ ★

The most poignant and powerful time for me in the film *12 Years A Slave* was not when the beatings took place or the general degradation meted out to the hero as a matter of course or even the general the terror of his life.

No. It is very quiet, very matter-of-fact: our hero is told that he will be called by another name from now on. He will no longer be Solomon Northrup.

He is now 'Platt', the name of a runaway slave from Georgia.

The name of someone else.

He is frightened, confused, beaten and humiliated, and now he must answer to another name.

A name given to him by someone else, a name given, ultimately, by conquest, a name that was not his choice, not his wish, a name that would be tied to him like the ropes that bound him and which he could not shake, could not undo – a name that would define him for ever.

He couldn't change/couldn't alter his reality.

At first he resists and demonstrates this by saying 'Solomon' when he is called 'Platt', but gradually he comes to learn that if he does not do as he is told, does not come when his new name is called, does not work, nor eat, nor sleep, nor run or play his fiddle or do nothing at all when he is commanded to under this new name, then the consequences for him could be dire . . . fatal.

In the end, he is freed His own name, the name he'd been born *because he does not* with, the name, I suspect, of his father, *forget his name.* had been thrown away, just as blithely as you blow away leaves or throw something into the trash. It was to be banished, never heard of again.

As 'Platt' the slave who ran away, Solomon Northrup has no ability to change his situation. He has no power.

In the end, he is freed because he does not forget his name.

★ ★ ★

We American, British, European Western peoples of West and Central African descent are here for one simple reason: our ancestors were brought here. Our identities, our customs and practices, our religions, our families, our dreams were taken away in order to feed a massive industry.

Scripture records that Adam named the animals: 'And Adam gave names to all cattle, and to the fowl of the air, and to every beast in the field.'

We may have been stripped of our names on the way down to the Atlantic coast to the ships or in the holding pens at the slave fortresses that dot Ghana's coast or perhaps we were stripped of our names on board the ships of our captivity, ships that were named *The Lord*, *The Ann* – owned by the United States Senate – and *The Good Ship Jesus*, one of the first slave ships ever built, and purchased from the Hanseatic League by Henry VIII.

It was necessary to take away our identities because once that is successfully done to a person or to a people, once it is impossible to alter your circumstances, your reality, to master your life and your fate and the fate of those you love, then the process of captivity, of enslavement – both physical and mental – can begin.

We are human beings, and we name things.

Scripture records that Adam named the animals: 'And Adam gave names to all cattle, and to the fowl of the air, and to every beast in the field' (Genesis 2.20 AV).

Naming is one of the key elements of our ordering of the world, of our placing ourselves in the world. Because, if we have our own names, that key to the citizenship of ourselves, then we can be free. We can be free to say 'yes', to say 'no' or to say nothing at all.

It becomes our choice.

We don't really know what trauma has been passed down from generation to generation, what the mental and emotional scars are that have been left upon us; our inheritance as the descendants of people who were treated less than human.

We don't know the full price paid for this trauma, and I'm not sure that anyone's ever measured it.

If not, one reason it hasn't happened is because no one concerned has had the ability to make it happen, has the power to create the systems where something so delicate, so subtle, so hidden could be brought out, and measured and defined and published – can be named.

And so, in some ways, black people in the West are not citizens of that first important nation: oneself.

We have not been allowed to say 'yes' or 'no' or nothing at all.

Yes, there is power, too, in not speaking.

Back to the Bible . . .

After he is whipped and tortured and crowned with thorns, Christ is brought before Pontius Pilate.

We can imagine the Prefect's annoyance.

Here he is, caught up in the midst of the most important, most emotional festival in the Jewish year, a time when all kinds of people have come to Jerusalem, a time when the streets are busier than ever, a time when tensions run high, everything and everyone is in a frenzy.

Pilate knows that the people out there in the streets want their nation back. He knows that they feel it is not for him to determine if they can make a go of it or even have the right to try.

But Rome has the say, the power; Rome is The Power.

It has the ability to exert its will, create its own reality. Answer yearnings and demands that suit the interests of Rome.

It will do as *it* sees fit.

So standing before Pontius Pilate is this half-dead, practically naked rabble-rouser, another one of those troublesome 'messiahs'; another person who believes he can take his destiny into his own hands, that he can help be a part of his people attaining their freedom. Pilate must feel that this man before him is, at the very least, a madman and, at worst, seditious.

After all, this street preacher has driven a tax collector away. He's entreated others to follow him, even though what he says seems ridiculous, unattainable, pointless. And he, Pilate, will demonstrate it now.

The Scriptures say (paraphrasing John 18.37) that Pilate asks, 'Are you a king?' And Jesus answers: 'You say that I am a king. I say that: I was born and came into this world to testify to the truth. Everyone on the side of truth can hear me.'

And then Pilate asks him, 'Quid est veritas? What is the truth?'

And the Scriptures say that Jesus does not answer.

Jesus does not answer.

Is it because Pilate's profound question is not really sincere and therefore not worthy of an answer?

All human beings are born into this world with the right to shape their reality, to live on their own terms in peace and in harmony with their fellow humans and nature.

Or is it because the Lord has the power in this situation, that he, even at this lowest ebb, can control his reality, make happen what is necessary, in his case, to continue his ministry, to continue to fulfil the prophecies, even in this condition, and in this place of pain and humiliation? Even now Jesus is teaching and healing, continuing to show that those in charge can be resisted.

And that all human beings are born into this world with the right to shape their reality, to live on their own terms in peace and in harmony with their fellow humans and nature.

And every human being has the right, the power, not to answer.

★ ★ ★

One of the definitions of the word 'power' is the ability to control people or things or a situation.

In our language it is taken from the Anglo-French *pouer*, 'to be able', which comes from the Vulgar Latin *potēre*.

The word 'power' is Middle English and its first known use was in the thirteenth century.

I don't think that this is an accident.

'Power' came into common usage around the time of Edward I, known as 'The Hammer of the Scots'. A man who crushed a nation.

The American southern states – before their defeat in the Civil War – were collectively known as 'The Slave Power'.

'Power' in our language gets born as the domain of the strong, of those who have the better weapons or technology, a larger population, who are rich – those who can change reality to suit themselves.

For it is they, in the end, who claim the right to name. Only they can determine the terms of engagement. Of reality.

And Jesus, silent before Pilate, teaches us that power need not rest in the ability to dictate the reality of another person or the ability to control a nation determined to define its own destiny in its own time.

Power can live inside, in the quiet assurance of allowing others to name themselves and not answer to a name or a condition that is not themselves.

Christ's answer to Pilate's question – 'What is truth?' – is silence.

And in that silence is a statement louder than words: it is the right to define who and what we are on our own terms.

It is the power to name ourselves.

WEEK TWO: NAMES
QUESTIONS FOR REFLECTION

- What are the various 'names' you go by? Mum? Dad? Sister? Brother? Doctor? Teacher?
- What do you make of the statement that those with power can 'claim the right to name'? How, if at all, does this inform our understanding of God as ultimate authority?
- Bonnie Greer says that 'power can live inside'. Where in the Bible do we see examples of this being the case?
- Read Isaiah 56.5. How does this passage reinforce the power of names?
- Bonnie Greer also talks about the power not to answer to names that are not our own. Can you think of a circumstance in which you have had to reject a 'name' someone else tried to put on you?

ONE OF THE GREAT . . .
LESSONS OF GOOD FRIDAY
IS THAT WE MUST BE
PREPARED TO LET PEOPLE
DOWN . . . IF BY DOING SO
WE DO WHAT IS RIGHT.

Week Three: Goodness

Ann Widdecombe

First broadcast on BBC Radio 4 on 12 March 2008

The Rt Hon. Ann Widdecombe, DSG, *is a former Conservative MP for Maidstone. She served as an MP from 1987 to 2010 and was also a member of the Conservative Christian Fellowship. Ann has presented documentaries, was the subject of a Louis Theroux profile and has appeared on* Strictly Come Dancing, *among other television shows. She is an accomplished author, with several novels, autobiographies and works of non-fiction to her name, including* Sackcloth and Ashes *(Bloomsbury Continuum, 2013).*

One of the sharpest pains we can endure is watching others suffering because we are suffering. The man dying in agony of an incurable disease will be as distressed by the emotional sufferings of his family as he is by his own physical ones. However unavoidable the disease, he will feel that he has somehow let them down, has deserted them.

How much sharper that pain becomes when the suffering is caused by a deliberate act. The bewilderment in the children's eyes and the misery in his wife's will haunt many a prisoner long after he has forgotten what the foreman of the jury looked like.

If either the sick man or the felon could miraculously take away the sufferings his condition was causing his nearest and dearest, then can there be any doubt that he would immediately do so?

When we think of Calvary, we think principally of the hideous suffering of a Roman crucifixion, of a slow death lasting for hours without even a millisecond's relief from pain. Perhaps also we think of the humiliation: the degrading dragging of the cross through the streets, the jeering crowds, the mocking soldiers, the gloating Sanhedrin. We marvel at the courage of the victim who forgave the perpetrators, enduring such agony without complaint.

And His mother watched it all, noticing every twitch of agony, hearing every unuttered groan, each stab of His pain an arrow through her own heart. Inwardly she must have been crying 'Why?' She would have remembered the angel who announced the conception of this special child, the One she had borne in a stable, had protected by fleeing to Egypt, had loved and nurtured until He became a man. Was this all it was for? For this shame and terrible, unspeakable agony?

And as she watched Him so He watched her watching Him, understanding the sheer grief that consumed her, knowing she did not share His knowledge of the coming resurrection, she did not understand why He was dying in so dreadful a fashion. He could miraculously have taken that pain away. He could have come down from the cross, but did not. He let her suffer on because He knew that what He was doing addressed a greater wrong, served a greater cause, and eventually she too would rejoice in that death, however slow and agonizing.

As He was suffering He was taunted by onlookers suggesting that if He really was God then He could come down from the cross at once. One of the thieves crucified with Him offered Him the same temptation but nothing surely could have tempted Him as much as the natural urge to relieve the misery and suffering of His own mother.

'He saved others; Himself he cannot save', goaded the watchers (Matthew 27.42, AV). Mary must have been wondering why not. He knew why not and must have wished she could understand.

Mary would not have been the only sobbing, confused sufferer on that first Good Friday. There were also the apostles, then merely disciples. For three years they had followed a man whom the crowds adored and the authorities feared. Only a few days

He knew that what He was doing addressed a greater wrong, served a greater cause.

earlier the people had hailed Him and strewn palm leaves in His path, cheering Him to the echo. Now those same people had howled for His death and the quaking authorities had won.

It must have baffled them, Peter, Andrew, James, John and all the others. Above all they must have felt so very badly let down. This was the man Who had performed all those miracles, had walked on water, Who had even raised the dead. Yet now He seemed helpless. Was it such a short while ago they had argued among themselves who would have the most important place in His Kingdom? So where was that Kingdom now the King himself was dying, defeated and scorned?

Some of them might have had different hopes. They might have believed Jesus was going to rid their land of the Roman invader, become a king, the long-awaited Messiah who would free his people from Caesar as Moses had freed them from Pharaoh – but without the inconvenience of wandering in the desert for 40 years.

Others may have had less specific but equally happy expectations.

To be with Jesus was to be with the winner, with a man who caused crowds to sit spellbound for hours as He preached, who could cure any ill, who so satisfyingly routed the Pharisees in debate. Now He had let them all down, was leaving them to go back to whatever it was they had been doing before He called them. The glory, the hope, the expectation, the devotion were over. It would hardly be surprising if they were angry as well as gloomy.

Some speculate that Judas may have betrayed Him in order to force His hand, confident that he was bringing forward the hour of Jesus' triumph. So shattered was he by the very different outcome that he took his own life.

Then there were the ordinary people. Those who had called for Barabbas to be released instead of Jesus might have been ruing their action. Those who had bravely called for Jesus would have been feeling let down. This man, they would have thought, was not, after all the Messiah, just another rash fool who had upset those with the power to crush him and who now left them with no hope, no solace, no expectation of some wonderful event to leaven the grind of their daily lives. Some would have shrugged, some wept, some sworn, some would have felt pity for the forlorn figure on the cross and others would have cursed Him for fooling them. All would have felt forsaken.

Of course Christ Himself knew what it was to be let down. His best friends fled at the moment He was being seized. He was betrayed by, of all things, the kiss of a follower. He listened while the man closest to Him swore by everything that was sacred he did not know Him. That, however, was different because so much of it was involuntary. His friends ran for cover because they were scared. Peter may have been a lying coward but he had at least crept along to see what was happening rather than desert his master altogether. Jesus knew they behaved from weakness only, but His own behaviour was that of full intent. He knew what He was doing, had the power to act differently, but resolutely held to His course.

Jesus knew they behaved from weakness only, but His own behaviour was that of full intent. He knew what He was doing, had the power to act differently, but resolutely held to His course.

He could have put an end to all their anxieties. He could have, even at the last minute, confounded Pilate and all the Roman officials, defeated the machinating Jewish authorities, restored the crowd's faith in Him. Yet He did not. He knew what those he loved expected of Him, knew what was right and knew the two things were different.

One of the great, perhaps often overlooked, lessons of Good Friday is that we must be prepared to let people down, to disappoint those whom we love, to refuse to live up to the expectations of others if by doing so we do what is right.

It is a test that confronts most of us in minor ways all our lives: the decision to follow the right course rather than the one others may expect, to stand out against the wishes of family, friends, workmates, political party, to be an irritant rather than conform.

For most of us the test is, mercifully, not so harsh or demanding as the one facing Jesus. Yet looking those we love in the eye and deliberately disappointing them when we have a choice to do otherwise is still one of the most difficult things we have to do.

He knew what those he loved expected of Him, knew what was right and knew the two things were different.

The child of a traditional Asian family in which she has been deeply loved, who decides she does not want an arranged marriage faces pressure much greater than any her family can bring to bear: that of the knowledge and guilt of hurting and disappointing those she loves. She looks into her mother's tortured eyes as Christ looked into the eyes of Mary as she wept by the cross.

The politician who takes a stand on an issue that is so contrary to his party's that it must deny him the successful career on which his friends and loyal supporters had relied. The whistle-blower who calls down opprobrium on the very people she works with daily, the parents who finally betray a criminal child to the police, the child with the strength not to follow friends into something forbidden, and so many others in so many situations, are making the choice to disappoint, hurt and bewilder family or friends or just those who rely on them.

For some people the dilemma appears in vastly more dramatic form and can shape history.

'Oh for goodness' sake, do what the king asks and come home', begged the wife of St Thomas More, unable, in her love and distress, to understand the principle that drove him to prefer the Tower of London and execution.

'For goodness' sake, Winston, let it alone. People don't want another war.' This was the sentiment confronting Churchill when standing against appeasement in a country that was still recovering from the devastating effects of the First World War. It was an opinion that would have been uttered not in irritation alone but out of concern, out of friendship, out of feeling for Churchill. And he looked his friends in the eye and said 'No.'

'Yes, of course it's awful what they are doing to Jews but, darling, you mustn't get involved. Think of the children. Do you want the SS coming for them?'

We should each ask what answer we would give to that last question. Because the hard truth is that the ultimate in letting down is not merely to desert but actively to put at risk those we love.

And the legacy of Calvary was just that. After His ascension, Christ left behind a collection of followers and their families who were never again to feel safe. Indeed, the very friend who swore so volubly that he did not know Him was himself to be crucified after years of defying the authorities in the name of Christianity.

Nor is it only the early Christians who suffered for their faith. Today there are parts of the world in which Christians are routinely persecuted, where conversion to Christianity can put the person at risk of imprisonment or even death. Each year, Christians die on the mission field, a much underappreciated fact of modern life.

But that, of course, is the extreme test. There are lesser ones that many confront daily; for example, standing up for Christian teaching in the face of work pressures to do otherwise, sometimes even at the risk of the livelihood itself.

If such people settle for a quiet life, preferring the happiness of family and the respect of friends over their own sense of right and wrong, then the world will be poorer. Without the willingness of Jesus Christ to let others suffer the most extreme misery for His sake and without His steadfastness of purpose in the face of that suffering, there would have been no salvation, no hope of eternal rest, no reconciliation of God and man. That would have been the price of coming down from the cross before the sacrifice was completed.

We might reflect that it was carried out by a man Who was all compassion, all caring, Who understood suffering and identified with the poor and oppressed.

Therefore, during this Lent, as we prepare both for Calvary and the resurrection by enduring some trifling penance of our own, we should perhaps look beyond the nails, the scourge, the crown of thorns, the thirst, the muscles aching with the unbearable pain, the jeering and the mockery and instead think of what then appeared as the greatest let-down of all time and of its utterly deliberate nature. Then we might reflect that it was carried out by a man who was all compassion, all caring, Who understood suffering and identified with the poor and oppressed.

Let us think of Mary watching Him and of Him watching her watching Him and know that this was by no means the least part of that great sacrifice: that one of the most important examples He left us was to look those we love in the eye and, in the full knowledge of the hurt we cause, to let them down.

WEEK THREE: GOODNESS
QUESTIONS FOR REFLECTION

- Can you recall a time when your suffering caused another to suffer alongside you? How did it feel?
- Ann Widdecombe mentions some of the things we associate with Calvary – crucifixion, humiliation, courage; what else might you add to this list?
- Can you imagine what it would be like to be in Mary's shoes? What would you think?

- Jesus went to the cross because he knew of God's bigger plan for humanity. Read Jeremiah 29.11. What solace can we take from knowing that God has a bigger plan for our lives as well?
- Do you feel like there are areas of your life in which you are doing the expected thing rather than the right thing? How might we start to address these areas this Lent?

HERE WAS THE IDEA THAT
ONE MIGHT DO SOMETHING
FOR OTHER PEOPLE, EVEN
TO THE POINT OF GIVING UP
YOUR OWN LIFE.

Week Four: Sacrifice

Giles Fraser

First broadcast on BBC Radio 4 on 31 March 2010

Giles Fraser is a Church of England priest, journalist and broadcaster. He is currently the parish priest at St Mary's Newington, and writes a weekly column for the Friday edition of The Guardian *as well as appearing frequently on BBC Radio 4. He is a regular contributor on* Thought for the Day *and a panellist on* The Moral Maze.

Holy Week is a searching audit of our moral courage. During this Holy Week, those of us who claim to be followers of Jesus Christ are invited, through the Passion story, to walk beside Jesus as he approaches his trial, suffering and death. It's always an intensely unsettling time, not least because the story forces us to face the fact that many of us may have more in common with those who betrayed Christ, and those who ran away, than with those who stood by him. Holy Week is a searching audit of our moral courage.

This year, this Passion story has been given a particular relevance for me by the fact that, during the last several weeks, I've been in the process of seeking to join the British army as a Territorial Army Chaplain. Just before Lent began, I went off to Army Office Selection Conference. After a muddy weekend of map reading, interviews and tying poles together with ropes, I got a letter saying that I was being offered a commission. This prompted a whole flood of emotions, mostly a combination of Boy's Own-type excitement and deep-down anxiety. And

Would my faith have survived the first-hand experience of so much suffering?

then, just a few days ago, after having pondered the prospect of deployment to Afghanistan – of how I'd cope, how my family would cope – I was given the news that, because I'm slightly asthmatic, I had failed my medical. And so, it seems, I'm not going to be joining the army after all. A part of me feels extremely disappointed and another part of me extremely relieved.

The idea was that I might become a chaplain to one of the Territorial Army field hospitals. So, throughout Lent, I've been thinking quite a lot about the pastoral care I'd be required to offer those who've been traumatized by the experience of death and horror. Inevitably, these thoughts have had a Lenten inflection. Not least, would I have had the guts to do what was being asked of me? Would my faith have survived the first-hand experience of so much suffering?

My interest in the army started several years ago when I was invited to lecture on ethics and leadership at the Defence Academy in Wiltshire. My previous experience of teaching ethics had been mostly of clever and slightly bored undergraduates for whom the big questions of life were sometimes little more than an opportunity to demonstrate intellectual sophistication. In contrast, at the Defence Academy I was giving lectures to hundreds of army officers, the majority of whom had seen combat experience in Iraq, and all of them wanted to think extremely hard about how questions of right and wrong found a place in what they'd been asked to do.

And the truth is, I was impressed. There was something about the way these men and women approached their task that thoroughly challenged my perception of what being in the army was all about. Of course, on one level I've always known that these young people had been risking their lives in the service of others, but I don't think I'd ever fully appreciated the extent to which soldiering requires selflessness.

As a schoolboy I learnt by heart Wilfred Owen's famous poem 'Dulce et Decorum est'. Having witnessed the horrors of the First World War, Owen described the idea that it is good and right to die for one's country as an 'old lie'. Words like 'honour', 'valour' and 'sacrifice' were the cornerstones of this old lie, for these were words that had the outward appearance of morality but had sucked a whole generation down into a pit of blood and darkness. Words like 'sacrifice' were so stained with suffering that they were not to be casually bandied about.

But the idea of sacrifice actually needs a fuller hearing than this. Consider, for instance, the sacrifice of those people who give up their social life, perhaps even their job, to care for a frail, elderly relative. People like this present an everyday example of sacrifice, very clearly putting the needs of another before their own. And most of us would recognize this as the very essence of moral goodness. Indeed, I would want to say that it's the very essence of the Christian gospel. Of course, in one way it sounds odd to say that this same order of moral goodness can be found on the field of battle, for the place where men and women kill each other is unquestionably a place of great evil. Yes, war is evil, but, as Prospero says to Miranda in *The Tempest*, 'What seest thou else . . .?'

'Greater love hath no man than this, that he lay down his life for his friends.' It is, of course, a reference in John's Gospel to Christ's death on the cross, but, chiselled into countless war memorials, it's also a phrase extensively borrowed to refer to the sacrifice of soldiers in war, reminding us that sacrifice is primarily this moral quality: a preparedness to put others first, their interests ahead of your own, even to the point of death.

There are some, of course, who say that today's younger generation has lost touch with these values, obsessed as it is with the shallow 'me first' celebrity lifestyles of overpaid footballers and trashy pop stars, but I just don't buy that at all. For, actually, as often, it's the young who are being asked to make these extraordinary sacrifices. Sure, people join up for a whole host of reasons – sometimes because it's the best way to escape a difficult background. Even so, there's no getting round the fact that it is largely the young who are coming back from Southern Afghanistan permanently disabled or not coming back at all. It is the young who are setting the rest of us so fine an example of moral courage.

And, yes, they do represent a profoundly countercultural challenge to a way of life that regards the cultivation of our own needs as the only worthwhile end in itself. For surely too often we find within modern life a suspicion of anything that has a call on our loyalty which is not directly bound up with our own immediate needs. You're deemed a sucker if you put the interests of others before your own. You're being used and manipulated. In this way, we are encouraged to emphasize the baser motives of other people as a way of excusing ourselves the responsibility for their care. 'Why should I look after her? She wouldn't look after me' – thus says the corrosive spirit of continual suspicion, a suspicion that gnaws away at our common life.

What so attracted me to the army was the complete absence of this sort of cynicism. Here was the idea that one might do something for other people, even to the point of giving up your own life. Believing these values to be so very important, I felt I couldn't stand by on the sidelines and just teach; I wanted to offer more practical support. Yes, to do my bit, to stand up and be counted.

But as soon as you've made this commitment, the question of courage hits you like a steam train. I was once shot at by the Israeli army in southern Gaza. Even though I was in the company of several small children at the time, I ran flat out to the nearest shelter, hoping everyone else had done the same, but not looking back to see. I have never been especially proud of how I reacted on that day. During Lent I've been asking myself whether or not I'd be more courageous if something like this were ever to happen to me again. How do people who don't feel blessed with huge resources of natural courage come to do what is right even when they're frightened? That, of course is the moral courage challenge of Holy Week.

Part of the answer to this challenge has something to do with practice, for the reason why armies have traditionally placed so much emphasis on repetition is that once you're able to do something again and again, almost without thinking, you're much more likely to be able to do it right in stressful situations, such as when you're under fire. I think there is something similar here in the moral life.

The great philosopher Aristotle argued that we come by our virtues via a process of habituation. This involves the surprising idea that, in order to become a better person, the first thing to do is act like a better person. Walk in the shoes of the person you want to become. Act it out first, acquire the right habits and your behaviour will eventually shape your character.

One of the important things about going to church a lot is that it does act a bit like a deliberate rehearsal for doing things right. The repetition of our theology in prayer and ritual and music are ways of keeping us true to what we profess to believe, shaping our affections and character, sculpting our identity so that we might be better prepared for what life might throw at us.

This idea of how we might grow in moral character is not one that makes much sense to those who assume the things we have to get right first are how we are or how we feel inside. This common way of presenting things assumes that moral change, the development of courage or becoming more sensitive to others, for instance, is generated from the inside out. From this perspective, the idea that you might change first by altering how you behave looks insincere, almost hypocritical, but it isn't.

This was the fascinating subject of a number of letters and poems written by the German pastor Dietrich Bonhoeffer from his prison cell in 1944. Bonhoeffer had been imprisoned by the Nazis for his hostility to their regime and was eventually to be hung at Flossenburg concentration camp in Bavaria in 1945 for his involvement in the plot to assassinate Hitler. In the long period in which Bonhoeffer was awaiting trial, he wrote much about the nature of moral courage and specifically about the relationship between his outward calm and his inner panic. In a poem called 'Who am I?', he would compare his inner turmoil and trembling with the person others described as confidently stepping from his cell 'like a squire from his country house'. To himself he felt like a 'contemptibly woebegone weakling' – that is how he described it – but to others he was clearly the very model of confidence and self-assured courage. Which one is the real me, he wonders in his poem? Does this huge gap between the confident outer me and the terrified inner me make me some sort of hypocrite? Perhaps is my inner weakling just the last vestiges of a retreating cowardice, a cowardice that is defeated by the way I outwardly conduct myself?

This is the question that has always obsessed those who face the prospect of battle. Is my inner fear evidence of cowardice? Will I have the guts to do what is right and what is expected of me? It's also the question that is at the heart of this Holy Week. Referring to his death, Jesus asked his followers, 'Can you drink the cup I am going to drink?' (Matthew 20.22 NIV) They all blithely said 'Yes', but when the time came, they ran away. What makes me think I will be any different? Most of us want to be good people and to do the right thing, but what will we actually do when we are far from home and scared out of our wits?

What I've been saying is that there is just half an answer to this question. For although we can never fully know how we will behave in stressful situations, what many of the great psychologists and philosophers say – as well as those who have practical experience of leadership in war – is that *in extremis*, we are the people we have practised to be. Moral courage and 'doing what is right' are not to be understood as isolated instances of right judgement calculated at the precise moment at which a decision is called for. In truth, when we get to what looks like the decision-making bit, most of the material for making that decision is already well in place. We are what we have practised to be.

So although it now looks as if I'm not going to be joining the army after all, I have certainly learnt a valuable lesson over these last several weeks. There is no way of knowing in advance how courageous any of us will be when seriously tested, but we considerably improve the odds of doing the right thing in difficult circumstances by finding ways to practise doing it when it's a lot easier – today, tomorrow.

In the Armed Forces' operational prayer book there's a prayer for courage in battle: that God will give me the strength to live up to all that I am called to be. It's not a bad prayer for Holy Week either.

WEEK FOUR: SACRIFICE
QUESTIONS FOR REFLECTION

- Giles Fraser explores various acts of selflessness. What day-to-day acts of others inspire you to this sacrificial living?

- Giles Fraser links courage with practice. In what areas of your life are you in need of courage this season? What patterns of practice could you put in place to help you rise to the challenge?
- How can we walk in the shoes of the people or person we want to become?
- Giles Fraser speaks of the repetition of church as being a good thing. Do you agree? Why?
- The Armed Forces' operational prayer book asks 'that God will give me the strength to live up to all that I am called to be'. What specific things do you feel God is calling you to this Lent?

IT'S NOT SIMPLY A
YEARNING FOR THE PAST
– IT'S A RECOGNITION OF
WHAT WAS GOOD IN THE
PAST AND WHAT HAS BEEN
LOST. THAT, I THINK, IS
SOMETHING SHE NEED NOT
APOLOGIZE FOR.

Week Five: Abandonment

Alexander McCall Smith

First broadcast on BBC Radio 4 on 27 February 2013

Alexander McCall Smith, CBE, FRSE, is a British writer and Emeritus Professor of Medical Law at the University of Edinburgh. He is internationally known as a writer of fiction, with sales of English-language editions exceeding 40 million and his books having been translated into 46 languages. He is most widely known as the creator of The No. 1 Ladies' Detective Agency series.

Every so often we read a report about the discovery, in some remote village somewhere, of the last speaker of a language. Of the 6,000 or so languages that exist in the world, it is estimated that around 500 are endangered, having only a small number of elderly native speakers left. Ultimately, for all of these it will come down to one person being left, as happened to Boa Senior, the last speaker of the Andamanese language, Aka-Bo, who died in 2010. Her death brought to an end one of the world's oldest languages. She was described, by a scholar who befriended her, as very lonely. I can imagine that. A whole world dies when a language becomes extinct: words for plants and animals, oral folklore, songs

– everything. The death of a language is the death of a whole way of looking at the world and of being.

As a novelist, I find myself drawn to the lives of those who must feel abandoned because the world has somehow moved on and left them stranded, either geographically or psychologically. The theme of abandonment, of course, has been a rich mine for novelists. Paul Scott's well-known novel, *Staying On*, is about an elderly British couple who stay on in India after Independence. They're stranded by history – abandoned, in a way, by the Raj that gave them their position and purpose. Now they're at the mercy of a new India that has, it seems, no place for them. How are they to maintain their dignity when everything they were used to is being discredited or dismantled? Time and history have conspired, it seems, to rearrange the furniture of their lives.

> *As a novelist, I find myself drawn to the lives of those who must feel abandoned because the world has somehow moved on and left them stranded, either geographically or psychologically.*

Then there is Graham Greene, who was such a master of this sort of fiction that he actually became a literary territory – Greene-land as it has been called. Think of Greene's washed-up priests, his lonely colonial officials, his exiles of one sort or another – they all inhabit worlds that have in one way or another been left behind, abandoned.

I've been talking about what happens in novels and, you may wonder, 'Is he talking about himself too?' The answer is, 'Yes,

I suppose I am.' Like all authors, I give myself away every other sentence. What the characters think and feel is often what the author himself or herself thinks and feels. One may as well admit that!

In my Botswana novels, the central character, Mma Ramotswe, talks about the changes she's seen in her country during her lifetime. She talks about the old Botswana values, as embodied in the example of her father, the late Obed Ramotswe. Mma Ramotswe does not see all change as bad – far from it. She sees many positive things in what her country has achieved, but she certainly regrets – and is not afraid to admit this – that qualities such as consideration for others, the ethos of sharing and the notion of kindness to strangers have to an extent been replaced by the more selfish values of contemporary individualism and materialism. I think in her case it's not simply a yearning for the past – it's a recognition of what was good in the past and what has been lost. That, I think, is something she need not apologize for and nor, indeed, should we. I feel that way about Scotland when I see certain things which were good and valuable in Scottish culture being swamped by the tide of aggression and selfishness disfiguring our lives today. Sometimes people say to me that this is simple nostalgia. Well, there may be nostalgia at work, but is nostalgia always a bad thing? Isn't nostalgia an entirely natural feeling – a feeling of regret that has its reasons?

In one of my books Mma Ramotswe is remembering her father – 'Not a day goes past,' she says, 'not a day but that I think of my late Daddy.' On this occasion she's recalling, with great affection, the battered old hat that he habitually wore. One night, while he was walking home in their village of Mochudi, a wind blew up and lifted his hat from his head. In the darkness he is unable to find it and has to return home hatless.

The next day, the hat is found by somebody and placed in a prominent position on a wall so that it might be found by its owner. That moved Mma Ramotswe – the thought that someone might care enough to ensure that the hat be restored to its owner. Then she moves from this reflection to an observation about the contemporary world: 'That's the trouble,' she says, 'we don't care enough today about the hats of others.'

Of course, the feeling that the world is changing about you and the old certainties have been lost is definitely age-related. If there are three ages, as the title of Titian's famous painting *The Three Ages of Man* suggests, then in each of these ages our view of the world has certain defining characteristics. In youth, although we may realize that the world is not how we would like it to be, we are usually confident this will change once we get our hands on it. Change is something we welcome and look forward to – it doesn't threaten us because it's change that we feel we shall be able to control; and, anyway, it's likely to be for the better. With maturity we lose some of that desire to change everything and find the world generally fairly satisfactory because it's our contemporaries who are running things and they, usually, reflect our values and concerns.

So far so good. But then, when you arrive in your fifties, you begin to notice that things are not what they once were. You look back on life 20 years ago and reflect on how much better it was. It was easier to do things then – things were cheaper, there were fewer restrictions, and public values tended to match your own. No longer. Politicians begin to say surprising things. Things you took for granted can no longer be relied on. The world is getting more difficult and more alien. If you pick up your telephone to query a bill, you find yourself talking to somebody many thousands of miles away who will have no idea of where you are and who you are. A familiar feeling? I'm sure it is, if you are over 50. If you are older than that, then it is probably even more familiar.

In the season of Lent, a time of sombre reflection in the Christian calendar, we might consider for a moment how this affects people who think of themselves as Christians. They may not necessarily be people of firm faith; they may just be people who identify themselves in a very loose sense with Christianity. How do these people feel about the transformation of a society

The freedom to speak one's mind should never amount to licence to hurt or belittle others, but it's important, I think, to defend freedom of speech in a liberal and tolerant society.

that once unhesitatingly described itself as Christian into one that appears to have, at times, no sympathy for the Christian position – is even hostile to it? I imagine that many Christians – even in this loose sense – feel isolated and vulnerable, afraid in some cases to speak their minds for fear of ridicule or, in some cases, actual discrimination. Of course, the freedom to speak one's mind should never amount to licence to hurt or belittle others, but it's important, I think, to defend freedom of speech in a liberal and tolerant society.

My characters have views ranging from atheism or agnosticism, explicit or otherwise, to firm religious beliefs. Isabel Dalhousie, my Scottish moral philosopher, is a bit like me, I suppose, in that she finds it difficult to accept some of the central claims of Christianity, although she's certainly sympathetic to the notion of a spiritual life; whereas Mma Ramotswe in Botswana goes to church every Sunday.

I remember once being subjected to withering scorn by an interviewer in Canada for that and I had to point out to him – he'd never been in any African country – that had I made Mma Ramotswe an atheist, it would have been totally unrealistic, as a very large proportion of the population has a religious faith. And her faith is part of her. She doesn't talk about it, but it's there and it manifests itself, quite frankly, in love. I don't think there's anything wrong in that. Unfashionable, maybe, in a society that is relentlessly materialist, but surely not wrong.

I think there's a real danger that when a society abandons established beliefs because they no longer fit, or because they seem downright implausible, we end up with a situation in which nobody believes in anything very much and, more significantly, we lose our sense of living within a civilization. Now that word – civilization – is a controversial one, but it still has, I think, a lot of work to do. I have been much impressed by the defence of the concept of civilization undertaken by a Scottish philosopher now living in Australia, John Armstrong. A few years back he wrote a fascinating book on what civilization means and how important it is to have sense of that. I am not suggesting for a moment – and neither was he – that the only basis for civilization in this country can be a sense of Christian identity. I don't think that, but what I do think is, if we cut ourselves off from those roots of our culture, then we may end up being without any civilized values – without any sense of what we really want our society to be and, critically, of who we are. Lent's a time when these deep questions can be addressed.

Of course, there are plenty of people who speak about values – listen to the way fairness is stressed in political debates these days – but the problem is that, in order for values to have real impact, they have to be part of a coherent overall view, a system of beliefs, so to speak. The Christian message has a lot to say about fairness; it has a lot to say about social justice; and also about forgiveness. It may be that at the heart of Christianity there are things people today simply cannot believe. I can understand that objection – I myself cannot believe a lot of it – but it does not mean I don't understand the power of its message and its efficacy in providing a fine set of principles by which to live. If it does that in the context of religious practices, I see no great harm and I am happy to participate. Indeed, I think that, for many people, it's the only way the values can be secured: by attaching them to a central story, they can relate to and integrate them into their lives. People have always needed their myths because myths provide a context for lives that otherwise might seem meaningless and random. It's wrong, I think, and certainly intolerant, to say people cannot embrace beliefs that help them lead good and constructive lives. I've seen that happen in Africa.

The Christian message has a lot to say about fairness; it has a lot to say about social justice; and also about forgiveness.

I've seen many people, inspired by their Christian faith, devoting their lives to helping others in their pain, poverty or need. I admire that; those people are better than I ever could be. I want my books to say something about that because I really think it's something to be admired and applauded.

And on that, let's give W. H. Auden the last word. Auden, it might be remembered, was a poet who, after realizing that science and psychology did not have the answer to evil (the rise of Hitler taught him that), came back to a Christian position in his gravely beautiful poem, 'New Year Letter'. In another of his great poems, 'Streams', Auden celebrates water and its properties. Here is what he has to say about the kindness of water:

> . . . and dearer, water, than ever your voice, as if
> glad – though goodness knows why – to run with the
> human race.
> Wishing, I thought, the least of men their
> Figures of splendour, their holy places.

The least of men. Yes. The least of men must be wished just that.

WEEK FIVE: ABANDONMENT
QUESTIONS FOR REFLECTION

- Alexander McCall Smith begins by discussing themes of loss and nostalgia. Are there areas of loss in your own life with which you are struggling to come to terms? Can you identify the good and the bad in that longing?

- Which of Titian's 'three ages' do you identify with most: a passion for change; content with our context; or nostalgic for the way things were?
- Do you agree with Alexander McCall Smith's assertion that our society has transformed from one that described itself as Christian to one that could even be said to be hostile to Christianity?
- Read Matthew 5.11. Have you ever faced discrimination for what you believe? How do you view that in relation to this passage?
- Read Ephesians 1.5. How, if at all, does your view of abandonment change in the light of God's adoption?

IF WE DON'T KNOW WHO WE ARE, WE CAN'T KNOW WHERE WE ARE GOING.

Week Six: Vision

Nick Baines

First broadcast on BBC Radio 4 on 29 February 2012

Nick Baines *is the Bishop of Leeds, an author, broadcaster and blogger. His blog* Musings of a Restless Bishop *has pulled in nearly two million views since he began it in 2009. He is frequently asked to comment nationally on topical issues and is regularly heard on the* Chris Evans Breakfast Show *on BBC Radio 2 and* Thought for the Day *on Radio 4.*

Nearly 3,000 years ago a wise man put into words what should be blindingly obvious: 'Without a vision the people perish.' Of course, he didn't know that this would be quoted for the next few millennia in worlds and contexts he couldn't possibly have imagined. 'Without a vision the people perish.' It encapsulates what many commentators and ordinary people have been trying to articulate in a world that has changed radically in the last three or four years.

First of all, the financial crisis in the capitalist world has led to radical questioning of what really matters to human society – and on what values such a society should be built. And while

Ask anyone involved on the ground with homeless people, people being made homeless or those who live in fear of losing the little they have. It is a colder world today.

much anger and blame have been heaped on to the heads of bankers, their gambling acumen and their extravagant bonuses, the cost is increasingly being borne by the poor and the vulnerable. Ask anyone involved on the ground with homeless people, people being made homeless or those who live in fear of losing the little they have. It is a colder world today.

Whatever the causes of the crisis, however, many commentators think it has exposed the lack of a thought-through and commonly owned consensus about what we want our society to look like. Questions of justice, equity and value

So who and what are we for? That's the question which keeps raising its head behind all the practical debates.

have been raised and, as the Occupy movement has made inescapably clear, there is now a cohort of people who refuse to let business continue as normal without challenge and debate. People and institutions that would have ignored such challenges only a couple of years ago are now openly accepting the need for a recalibration of the relationship between labour and reward. So the world has changed – for the time being at least.

So who and what are we for? That's the question which keeps raising its head behind all the practical debates. It's not a new question but it has often been submerged under an acceptance of the status quo when all seems to be going well and we don't want to upset what is weirdly called 'normality'. However, 'normality' was further disrupted during the summer of 2011.

At the beginning of August my wife and I flew out of London for a holiday with friends in the United States. Not long after we arrived there I got a telephone call to say that there were riots in Croydon – the place where I had lived and been bishop until recently – and that our youngest son was holed up in his flat while the violence went on outside. Inevitably, then, we followed the news as, for many people in London, law broke down and the commentariat offered instant analyses of the causes.

Interpretation and judgement were instant – particularly in the media and from the mouths of those who can't resist the seduction of a microphone. One of the characteristics of the ensuing analysis was the charge that English society had lost any sense of a collective narrative. What does that mean? Quite simply, that we no longer know who we are, why we are here or what we are trying to become.

Now, that might sound a little philosophical and vague but it actually poses a serious challenge to the way we live – and the way we understand our common life. 'Without a vision the people perish' – or, as we might rephrase it, if we don't know who we are, we can't know where we are going.

Go back to the Old Testament and we find there a good illustration of this contemporary predicament. The Israelites had been liberated from oppressive exile in Egypt. They then wandered through the desert for 40 years while a generation of nostalgia merchants and moaners died off. Then, just before they entered into the land they believed they had been promised, they were given some stark and uncompromising warnings: when you settle and things begin to go well for you, you will forget that once you were slaves. And when you forget your story – your 'narrative' – you will begin to assume that all your wealth is down to your own efforts, and you will start treating other people as your slaves. If you lose the plot – literally – you will lose all that speaks to you of your identity. Life is not a game and people are not to be treated as pawns in the hands of those who assume the right to a personally comfortable life at the expense of others.

In fact, in order to ensure that the people didn't lose touch with their founding narrative, they were to instigate annual festivals – rituals designed to remind them (in body, mind and spirit) of the story that was to drive them as they shaped their society. Some of these rituals involved, for example, leaving the crops at the edges of your field so that asylum-seekers and the dispossessed could have something to eat. Or bringing the first (and best) 10 per cent of your crop to the priest, to whom you would then address a creed – not a simple statement of doctrine but a story that roots you and your community. This creed would begin with the statement, 'My father was a wandering Aramaean . . .'. In other words, the starting point of the story that defines us – that tells us who we are – is we are transient, we belong together, we journey together with responsibility for one another. Or to answer a different biblical question. 'Yes, I am my brother's keeper – and he is mine.'

What shocked many observers about the summer rioters' 24-hour holiday from civilization was the sense of disconnection from society – a rejection of any identification with what we might call 'the rest of us'. No investment in belonging to or shaping or taking responsibility for the community in which they live. No sense of obligation towards anyone else – and no concept of belonging to a community of accountability.

What would we say was the narrative that unconsciously drove these people? Every man for himself? The survival of the fittest? 'Me first' individualism? Or have they simply drunk too deeply of the wells of Hollywood in which the so-called 'myth of redemptive violence' is portrayed as self-evidently true and the only effective way of making sure no one gets one over on you?

I guess this brings us back to that question of narratives and vision. Just what sort of a society do we think we are creating? What sort of a community do we wish to become? What does our vision look like – or don't we have a common vision towards which we are working?

God, we learn, is rather concerned about justice and whether or not the poor are fed.

Well, that's where the debate begins for us. After all, we have to take responsibility for how we collectively and individually shape our vision and begin to earth it in the structures and stuff of social priorities. But the need to question and challenge our world view is unavoidable if we take the biblical narrative with any degree of seriousness. God, we learn, is rather concerned about justice and whether or not the poor are fed.

Which is where Lent comes in. Lent offers the space for reflection on what really motivates and drives us – what the values and core beliefs are that shape how we see and how we live with ourselves and one another; how we love and hate; who we love and hate. In other words, we are invited to take the trouble to work out within which – or whose – narrative we locate ourselves.

One of the problems for many of us is our assumed familiarity with the Gospels. Rather than being comforted by them, if we read them properly, we find ourselves deeply challenged – especially by the habit of God's people to lose the plot, forgetting their vocation to live and give their lives in order that the world should see who God is and what he is about.

At the beginning of Mark's Gospel we find Jesus returning from his baptism and testing in the desert and 'proclaiming the good news of God' in the hill country of the north, where he was from originally. This is summed up in four phrases: 'The time is now; God is present among you again; change the way you look at God, the world and us; now live differently in that world.' All right, that's a paraphrase, but it illustrates the dynamic of what Jesus was trying to do and say. We could put it like this: 'You have been praying for generations that God would be among you again, which you think he can't be while the "unclean" Roman occupying forces remain in your land, but dare to think differently. What if God broke his own rules and came into the contaminated space and contaminated it with hope and generosity and goodness? Just imagine. Can you dare to look differently at God, the world and us, even seeing God present in surprising, healing – even shocking – ways? Or can you only spot God's presence when everything is going well for you and all your problems have been resolved?'

In fact, in the Gospels we see this time and again. Before he launches out on his fatal mission of challenge, Jesus goes into the desert for 40 days and nights to face hard questions: Are you really willing to do this God's way – even if it ends on a cross? Are you going to be driven by the desire for quick glory – or can you really defy the god of self-preservation and lay down your life for the sake of the world?

This was real, hard, deep soul-searching – drilling down to what really motivated Jesus, to what was the fertile soil from which the rest of his behaviour would grow.

Going to the end of Luke's Gospel, we find the risen Jesus walking alongside a couple of bewildered and frightened disciples who couldn't make any sense of Jesus' having died – the Messiah wasn't supposed to do that. Having told their version of the story, which didn't add up, Jesus then retells it, enabling them to see God, the world and themselves differently – through a reshaped lens, as it were.

And that's the challenge for any one of us or any community thinking we take God and his invitation seriously. Not only am I as an individual required to reflect the Christ whose name I bear but I am also required to help shape my community or society accordingly. The rest of the Gospel narratives simply identify those who could or could not dare to change the way they looked at, saw, thought about and lived in God's world.

Then of course they drop on us the challenge faced by the first disciples of Jesus: to be changed and challenged as we walk with him from the shores of Galilee to a cross planted in the rubbish tip outside the city, through a grave and into a surprising future.

I suppose Lent offers us the opportunity to question again the vision that fires us and measure it against one we think we know – that of Jesus. This is the vision that captivated me as a teenager in Liverpool and has never let me go. As a young man I saw it in purely individual terms – a personal discipleship aimed at spiritual growth and personal holiness. The problem was that I then read the rest of the Bible and couldn't escape the insistent call to anyone who agrees to reflect the character of the God revealed there – that is, the call to give up one's life for the sake of others.

It's not a bad prayer for Lent, recalling us to a vision of generosity, self-giving and confident humility.

The irony, of course, is that this was always the call of God's people, but the temptation is always to get distracted by more comfortable – or less demanding – narratives and lose the plot.

The great Canadian singer-songwriter Bruce Cockburn wrote a beautiful song way back in 1976 called 'Lord of the Starfields' in which he sets the 'now' against the larger backdrop of the whole created order of the universe. The refrain comes as a simple prayer, encapsulating a vision for the here and now derived from a perception of eternity that shapes how we can be into the future: 'Love that fires the sun keep me burning.'

It's not a bad prayer for Lent, recalling us to a vision of generosity, self-giving and confident humility. Maybe even a vision that calls a broken society back from its immediate practical questions and poses a more fundamental challenge: for whom and for what are we here? And if our society seems too complicated to begin to think about such a conversion, then I recall that Jesus, in three short years, spent time with 12 people who never quite got it and yet through them changed the world.

WEEK SIX: VISION
QUESTIONS FOR REFLECTION

- Lent can be the perfect time to reflect on our own vision: who and what are we for?
- How in touch with your 'founding narrative' would you say you are with regard to your beliefs? How does the past narrative shape your future vision?
- What does 'community' mean to you? In what different communities do you play a part?
- What sort of a community do we wish the Church to become? What is our vision?
- As Nick Baines asks, 'Can you dare to look differently at God, the world and us, even seeing God present in surprising, healing – even shocking – ways? Or can you only spot God's presence when everything is going well for you and all your problems have been resolved?' Perhaps this Lent we can open our minds up to be surprised by God afresh.